OWLS

A PORTRAIT OF THE ANIMAL WORLD

Paul Sterry

TODTRI

This book was designed and produced by
Todtri Productions Limited
P.O. Box 20058
New York, NY 10023-1482
Fax: (212) 279-1241

Printed and bound in Singapore

ISBN 1-880908-31-X

Author: Paul Sterry

Producer: Robert M. Tod
Book Designer: Mark Weinberg
Photo Editor: Edward Douglas
Editors: Don Kennison, Shawna Kimber
Production Co-ordinator: Heather Weigel
DTP Associate: Jackie Skroczky
Typesetting: Command-O, NYC

Printed and bound in Singapore by Tien Wah Press

PHOTO CREDITS

Photographer/Page Number

Aquila Photographics
J. J. Brooks 59 (bottom), 60 (top)
John Carlyon 75 (bottom)
N.W. Harwood 61
Brian Hawkes 18 (tops)
Hanne & Jens Eriksen 40-41, 51 (top), 51 (bottom), 76 (bottom)
Wayne Lankinen 56-57, 66 (bottom), 69 (bottom)
C. Reddick 55
Reinhard Siegel 14, 31, 75 (top)
Bates Strathy 78
C & T Stuart 77 (bottom), 79
M. C. Wilkes 27 (top)

Dembinsky Photo Associates
Anthony Mercieca 23
Gary Meszaros 34 (top)
Skip Moody 16, 42
Alan G. Nelson 20, 70 (top)
Rod Planck 28, 29
A. B. Sheldon 32

Joe McDonald 5, 6, 10, 13, 22, 35, 36, 38 (top), 38 (bottom), 39 (top), 39 (bottom),
44 (bottom), 45, 46 (bottom), 47 (top), 48, 49, 52 (top), 52 (bottom), 59 (top), 60 (bottom), 64, 65

C. Allan Morgan 67, 69 (top), 76 (top)

Nature Photographers Ltd.
Hugh Clark 47 (bottom)
P. Craig-Gordon 74
R. S. Daniell 21
Michael Gore 12
E.A. James 46 (top)
Philip J. Newman 34 (bottom)
Roger Tidman 77 (top)

Leonard Lee Rue III 63 (bottom)

Gail Shumway 26, 30, 43, 44 (top), 53

Tom Stack & Associates
Larry Brock 11 (top), 17
Perry Conway 18 (bottom), 72-73
Jeff Foott 62 (top), 63 (top)
Thomas Kitchin 19
Kevin Schafer 37, 68
Wendy Shatil 24-25
John Shaw 11 (bottom)
Robert C. Simpson 8-9
Diana Stratton 66 (top)

The Wildlife Collection
Michael Francis 4, 71
D. Robert Franz 15, 54, 58
John Giustina 7, 33
Martin Harvey 27 (bottom)
H. Holdsworth 62 (bottom)
Robert Lankinen 3, 50, 70 (bottom)

INTRODUCTION

Intent on finding prey, this great grey owl is oblivious to the photographer. During winter months northern owls can become remarkably bold and easy to spot in daylight.

Dusk falls on the forest, and dying glimmers of sunlight are replaced by the faint glow of the moon. Beneath the canopy of leaves, life stirs on the woodland floor as the nocturnal inhabitants awaken and go about their daily business. It is autumn and amongst the leaf litter is a rich harvest of fallen nuts and fruits, attracting the interest of rodents—in particular, the wood mouse.

A youngster from one of this year's many litters of mice in the forest is keen to feast on these riches, and noisily rustles

amongst the leaves in search of acorns. Its movements do not go unnoticed, however. High above, resting quietly on an overhanging perch, a tawny owl scans the ground below, its pronounced senses of vision and hearing acutely honed and focused.

The mouse scurries into view and without hesitation the owl glides silently toward the unsuspecting creature with talons outstretched. The talons bite into the unfortunate mouse and, with a single, powerful squeeze, life is extinguished. The owl then returns to its perch to swallow the meal whole. On a good night the owl may catch several small mammals, but if feeding is poor a single mouse can sustain this hardy predator for the duration of the night.

To anyone with a fanciful imagination an owl can seem to have an almost human face. Couple this appearance with their often blood-curdling calls and nocturnal habits, and it is perhaps not surprising that these birds feature frequently in mythology and superstition. To some cultures they are symbols of wisdom while to others they represent malevolent spirits or harbingers of doom and death. That they were important in Greek mythology can be noted by the genus name Athene (e.g., the little owl and its allies). Owls also appear often in Chinese legends, as well as in the folklore of Medieval Europe and subsequent eras of western culture.

A lightweight body in relation to wing area enables this long-eared owl to convey buoyant flight. Excellent night vision allows it to avoid obstacles such as branches as it swoops through the trees.

Scanning its territory for prey, this northern hawk owl is using the tallest pine tree in the vicinity. The precise distribution of this species is rather unpredictable due to fluctuations in numbers of prey animals such as lemmings.

OWLS OF THE WORLD

Despite varying in size from a length of about 10 centimetres (4 inches) to over 70 centimetres (28 inches), and boasting a wide range of markings, all owls are easily recognised as belonging to the same group and sharing similar characteristics. Most distinctive of these is the appearance of the head, with its flattened, forward-facing facial disc surrounding relatively large eyes. In most species the plumage appears as rather subdued shades of brown and grey, with feather patterns that often provide amazingly proficient camouflage for daytime roosts.

What is an Owl?

Owls are predators which, by and large, specialise in catching ground-dwelling small mammals; birds, reptiles, insects, and earthworms are also taken by some species. Although they share their feeding habits with diurnal birds of prey, they are not in any way related to predators such as eagles,

Following page: With just its face in view at the entrance to its nest hole, this screech owl has a distinctly cat-like appearance. Tree holes are commonly used by many owl species as nest sites.

Wing-spreading by this great grey owl indicates that an attack is imminent. A single blow from the talons can easily draw blood and leave a deep gash in the skin of the intruder.

Keeping a watchful eye on its nest, this great horned owl will not tolerate any potential predator's approach too close to its territory.

falcons, or hawks. Owls avoid competing with these birds by their largely nocturnal habits; more than 60 percent of the 134 known owl species feed after dark, and of the remaining 40 percent, few are exclusively diurnal. Given their feeding habits it is not surprising that they possess structural features in common with diurnal birds of prey: hooked bills used for tearing the flesh of their prey and powerful feet with sharp talons used for gripping.

Owls are an extremely wide-ranging classification of birds with many representative species occurring in almost all parts of the world where suitable prey animals can be found.

Classifications

Scientists classify owls as belonging to the order Strigiformes, a group which is most closely related to nightjars, potoos, cuckoos, and swifts. The order is divided into two families: the Tytonidae, or barn owls and related species, of which there are up to ten species known, according to which classification source is quoted; and the Strigidae, to which the remaining 124 owl species belong. The following survey comprises a selection of the most characteristic, striking, and best-known owl species from around the world.

Although mostly nocturnal in its habits, barn owls are occasionally seen flying in daylight hours, particularly in the late afternoon. Their leisurely, confident flight is easily observed.

Barn Owl

The barn owl *(Tyto alba)* and its relatives differ from more typical owls in a number of ways. Most strikingly the facial disc, rather than being rounded, is heart-shaped and this surrounds relatively small, dark eyes.

The barn owl is a most attractive species whose upperparts are a warm buffish brown, speckled with white and black. The face is white, as are the underparts; those found in mainland Europe have a buffish wash on the breast. The legs are long and white with wide-spreading toes and fearsome talons.

As its name suggests, the barn owl uses barns and other man-made structures for nesting and roosting during the daytime. At dusk the owls emerge to quarter the surrounding countryside for food.

Enlightened landowners view the barn owl as a friend. These birds kill large numbers of potentially damaging rodents such as rats and mice. Some people even create artificial nest platforms to encourage the owls.

11

As their common name suggests, barn owls are often associated with farm buildings, nesting amongst the rafters or indeed on specially constructed nesting platforms. Their preferred feeding habitats are rough fields and meadows although roadside verges are often favoured these days, their ghostly white shapes sometimes caught in passing car headlights. Barn owls feed primarily at night but are occasionally seen at dusk. They characteristically quarter up and down likely-looking areas for their main quarry—voles and mice—but will sometimes scan the ground from a lookout post.

The barn owl is one of the most widespread of all land birds. It occurs throughout most of Britain and Europe and across many parts of Asia, Africa, Australia, and in much of North America. In South America it is found in areas of suitable grassland, as well as on oceanic islands such as the Galápagos. The family is represented by several other species of *Tyto*, which are found around the world, and by the secretive bay owls (genus *Phodilus*): two species of this group are now known, one from south-east Asia and the other from Africa.

Scops Owl

The engaging Scops owl *(Otus scops)* is a common but easily overlooked bird of southern Europe, North Africa, and parts of western Asia. It is strictly nocturnal, roosting during the daytime amongst dense foliage; in this respect, its incredibly patterned plumage affords it a remarkable camouflage whose overall effect resembles tree bark. Two colour forms of the Scops owl are recognised, one of which is largely brown, the other mostly grey. They feed mainly on insects which may be caught in flight, taken from the ground, leaves, or on branches.

The Scops owl's most distinctive feature is its voice. Sounding for all the world like a sonar blip, the monotonous call is evocative of warm spring and summer evenings around the Mediterranean. The call is often the only clue to the presence of this owl. If seen well, however, the large staring yellow eyes and strangely angular head shape are striking. Like many species of owls, Scops owls are able to change shape quite markedly. By stretching or hunching their bodies they can appear tall and elongated, or squat and almost shield-shaped.

Staring orange eyes framed by black and white facial markings characterise the white-faced Scops owl. The owl is found in sub-Saharan Africa and is fairly common in Kenya.

Screech owls have a varied diet that includes small mammals, lizards, amphibians, and invertebrates. This one has captured a large moth, which will provide a nutritious meal.

Scops owls from the north of their range are migratory, moving to Africa in the winter, while those in some parts of the Mediterranean region and North Africa are resident. There are several other species of Scops owls found in many parts of the world with the exception of the Americas. Some species, especially those from oceanic islands and Africa, have extremely restricted distributions and are poorly known. The Sokoke Scops owl *(Otus ireneae)*, for example, is currently known only from one relict patch of tropical forest on the Kenyan coast.

Screech Owls

The group of species collectively known as screech owls is in many ways the American equivalent of Scops owls. Both belong to the genus *Otus* and the distinctions between them are rather arbitrary. One of the best-known species is the eastern screech owl *(Otus asio)*, which occurs in the east of North America from southern Canada to northern Mexico. Like the Scops owl, its colours are grey and brown, and its plumage affords it superb camouflage in its daytime roost.

A strictly nocturnal species, the eastern screech owl most often gives away its presence by its call, generally described as a tremulous wailing. It is the subject of numerous superstitions in rural communities and, as in many other parts of the world, a screech owl calling from the roof

of a house is thought to prophesy a death in the family.

Eastern screech owls favour areas of open woodland, farmland, and even mature gardens. They nest in holes in trees and feed mainly on insects and other invertebrates, as well as reptiles and the occasional small mammal. Across the western portion of North America the species is replaced by the western screech owl *(Otus kennicottii)*, a bird that is almost identical in appearance to its eastern counterpart but with a very different call. There are several other species of screech owls in South America; the most widespread is termed the tropical screech owl *(Otus choliba).*

Eagle Owl

With a length of nearly 70 centimetres (28 inches), the eagle owl *(Bubo bubo)* is one of the most impressive of all owl species. It is an extremely heavy and powerfully built bird with a large beak and huge talons. Not surprisingly, it is capable of killing prey the size of a small deer, although it more usually tackles hares, rabbits, and large birds.

The eagle owl's most striking features are its large, orange eyes. It has long ear tufts which are raised or lowered depending on the mood of the creature. The plumage is mostly brown and finely marked with darker blotches and barring. Across its extensive range, which embraces much of Europe with the exception of Britain, eastern Asia, and northern Africa, there is considerable variation in the hue of the ground colour, and thus in its plumage.

Although nocturnal in its feeding habits, eagle owls are sometimes located by careful searching with binoculars of likely roosting or nesting sites. Since these are invariably inaccessible rocky cliffs, gorges, or crags, there is little danger of disturbing the owls themselves. Despite their size, however, they can be extremely difficult to spot, and their presence is usually indicated first by hearing their loud and deep booming call, often rendered as 'boo-hoo'.

Visitors to East Africa stand a good chance of seeing Verreaux's eagle owls while on safari. Because of the confidence their size confers upon them, they are often seen during the daytime.

Great Horned Owl

The great horned owl *(Bubo virginianus)* is the New World equivalent of the eagle owl, and occurs in suitable habitats from northern North America down to the southern tip of South America. Although slightly smaller than its European counterpart, measuring roughly 50 centimetres (20 inches) in length, it is no less impressive. It has large, staring yellow-orange eyes, bordered in most races by an orange-buff facial disc. The plumage is beautifully marked and patterned with greys and browns, and the underparts in particular have delicate but striking barring.

Great horned owls are well known for their calls, which include loud and booming wails and hoots. In North America the owls are most vocal in February, the start of the breeding season.

Fishing Owls

As their name suggests, these owls are expert fish catchers that have effectively abandoned terrestrial mammals and birds as a source of food. There are three known species, all of which occur in Africa south of the Sahara, Pel's fishing owl *(Scotopelia peli)* the most frequently encountered. They characteristically feed by gliding down from an overhanging perch to grab a fish from the surface of the water. The owls are sometimes partly immersed during fishing forays, and all three species have unfeathered legs and feet, an adaptation to this feeding strategy.

Fishing owls are not to be confused with fish owls, a group of four species that belong to the genus *Bubo*, and are thus related to eagle owls and the great horned owl; they do, however, share these owls' large, staring eyes and long 'ear' tufts. Fish owls are found in Asia and, like their African counterparts, feed by making shallow plunge-dives for surface-feeding fish. The three tropical species of fish owls have unfeathered legs and feet.

A fearless hunter, the great horned owl will take large and active prey animals. This one has captured a rabbit, and is quite capable of flying off with its quarry locked in its talons.

Arguably the most impressive owl found in the Americas, the wide-ranging great horned owl is found throughout the region in suitable habitats. It gains its name from the hornlike feathers on its head.

In flight a snowy owl is an impressive sight. They will capture prey the size of snowshoe hares or ptarmigan with ease, usually taking their quarry by surprise.

Snowy Owl

Due mainly to their large size, essentially pure white plumage, and often diurnal habits, snowy owls *(Nyctea scandiaca)* are amongst the most easily recognised of all owls and can be instantly identified by most bird-watchers. There can be few more impressive sights than one of these huge owls gliding on large, rounded wings over the tundra or a wintery landscape.

As might be guessed by their white plumage, snowy owls are essentially northern birds which breed on the Arctic tundra, only moving south when forced to by the excessive cold and snows of winter. During the summer months, when daylight is almost continuous in the Arctic, they hunt for lemmings, other small mammals, and birds. During the winter months they continue to feed in daylight hours although the prey taken is necessarily more varied and dependent upon their location.

Seen at close range the snowy owl has piercing yellow eyes and a jet-black beak. As a protection from the cold, its legs and even the toes are feathered. Males, which are noticeably smaller than females, have pure white plumage whereas that of the female is speckled and barred with buff-brown; this provides useful camouflage when incubating eggs on the ground nest-site.

While female and immature snowy owls show barring on their feathering, the plumage of the male is pure white. Its camouflage in a wintery landscape can be astonishing.

Its huge size and white plumage make the snowy owl the most distinctive and easily recognisable of all owls. Sitting on the snowy tundra, it looks for all the world like a pale boulder.

Little Owl

As the name denotes, the little owl (*Athene noctua*) is a comparatively small species of owl, not much more than 20 centimetres (8 inches) in length. It is widely distributed, however, and occurs throughout most of Europe, including Britain, where it was introduced, as well as in North Africa and across the Middle East into western Asia.

Little owls hunt not only at night but also during the daytime. They characteristically perch on fence posts, telegraph poles, or in trees, scanning the ground below for likely prey. Their usual quarry includes insects and earthworms, as well as small mammals and birds if these can be caught. Little owls nest in holes in trees and, especially while nesting, make a weird array of catlike calls.

Pygmy Owl

Smaller still than the little owl, the pygmy owl (*Glaucidium passerinum*) is Europe's smallest owl, measuring just 17 centimetres (7 inches) in length. It is represented in different parts of the world by other closely related and very similar members of the genus *Glaucidium*; in North America, the species is termed the northern pygmy owl (*Glaucidium gnoma*).

The pygmy owl has a rather compact body but a relatively long tail, and its plumage is greyish brown with white spots on the upperparts. It is mainly a daylight feeder and is sometimes seen perched on a dead branch or fence post, scanning the terrain for prey. Animals taken include small mammals and birds, often as big as the owl itself.

Pearl-spotted Owlet

In many respects the pearl-spotted owlet (*Glaucidium perlatum*) is the sub-Saharan Africa equivalent of the pygmy owl, as it is much the same size and similar in appearance. Like its European counterpart it is often seen in the day, although it will hunt at night too. Pearl-spotted owlets are mainly insect feeders and regularly perch in acacia bushes. They have subtle pearl-spot markings on their plumage, and two large 'eye' markings on the back of the head, which presumably serve to distract or deter would-be attackers.

A diminutive pygmy owl perches on a spray of flowers. Despite its small size this species is an aggressive predator, capturing mainly birds, some of which may be almost equal in size to the owl itself.

The tiny pearl-spotted owlet is widespread in East Africa and often seen during daylight hours. Pairs are sometimes heard duetting by visitors on camping safaris.

Elf Owl

Measuring a mere 14 centimetres (5 inches) in length, the elf owl *(Micrathene whitneyi)* is the smallest species of the group. It is primarily a desert species and is frequently depicted peering out from a hole excavated in a large cactus. The owl does not create its own hole but instead takes one over that has been carved out by a woodpecker.

Elf owls are nocturnal birds, and a face at a nest hole is usually all a bird-watcher will see during the hours of daylight. After dark they take to the wing in search of ground-dwelling insects and hawk moths. Their range includes the south-western states of North America and northern Mexico.

Burrowing Owl

There can be few more engaging sights in the bird-watching world than a family of burrowing owls *(Athene cunicularia)* at the entrance to their nest burrow. Some of the youngsters will peer at onlookers from the mouth of the burrow while, at the surface, the parents will stare fixedly, sometimes bobbing up and down or even turning their heads upside down.

Burrowing owls are found in the Americas throughout North America and in parts of Central and South America with sparse vegetation. As their name suggests, they nest in burrows, which are sometimes excavated by the owls themselves, but are more usually

Following page: As if its staring eyes, hooked bill, and sharp talons were not intimidating enough, this young great horned owl adds to its off-putting appearance by fluffing itself up and arching its wings over its back.

Smallest of all owls, the elf owl is found in the southern United States, as well as in Central America. It favours desert habitats where it nests and occupies day-time roosts in holes in cacti and trees.

Lizards and grassland insects comprise a major part of the diet of the burrowing owl. The range of this species extends from the southern states of North America southward into Central and South America.

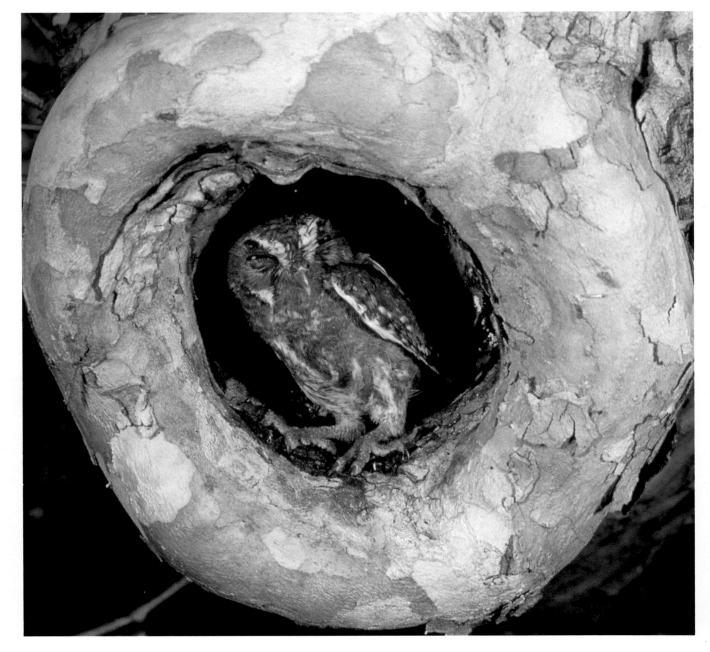

23

those abandoned by rabbits. They are comparatively easy to see, partly because they are often active in daylight, and partly because they are surprisingly bold and approachable. This is especially so in some parts of Florida where the owls nest on golf courses.

Tawny Owl

The tawny owl *(Strix aluco)* is certainly the most familiar of its kind in Britain, and also in parts of mainland Europe. The most widely distributed colour form is brown plumage that is richly marked with darker streaks and bars; races from the east of its range are more grey in appearance.

The tawny owl is strictly nocturnal and remains well hidden during the daytime.

After dark, however, its silent shape is sometimes seen in wooded clearings and its loud calls are a familiar sound to most people. There are numerous calls but the most common is the 'te-wit, te-woo', in fact a duet between two birds.

Tawny owls are primarily birds of the woodlands, although they are becoming increasingly common in urban settings. During the daytime they are sometimes discovered by smaller songbirds and mobbed and scolded mercilessly; keen-eared bird-watchers often use the alarm calls of these birds to find the owl too. The major part of the tawny owl's diet is comprised of small mammals such as mice and voles, although they will take earthworms and insects as well.

The tawny owl's mottled plumage affords it excellent camouflage at its winter daytime roost. If small birds find the owl, however, they will mob it noisily until it moves off.

Burrowing owls will sometimes excavate their own nest burrows, but more often take over or enlarge one previously dug by a rabbit. The burrows are some-times in seemingly unlikely sites such as golf courses or road-side embankments.

Great Grey Owl

During the winter months great grey owls often hunt during daylight hours. From a suitable vantage point, they scan the snow-covered ground below for signs of small mammals utilising both sight and sound to assist them.

The huge great grey owl *(Strix nebulosa)* is a bird of the northern forests and occurs at these high latitudes across much of northern Europe, northern Asia, and northern North America. For its size it is an elegantly proportioned bird with a most striking facial disc bearing concentric dark rings around the eyes; the plumage is mostly grey-brown with darker barring and streaks.

Great grey owls hunt mostly during the day; indeed, they have no option but to do so during the extended hours of daylight associated with northern summers. They feed mainly on voles and lemmings, and nest in abandoned nests of birds of prey or in hollow tree stumps. As some foolhardy bird-watchers have come to know, great grey owls will vigourously defend their nest and young, unhesitatingly attacking with their talons.

Excessive cold and a poor supply of prey animals may force northern owl species such as this great grey owl to move south. In a snow-clad landscape they stand out clearly to bird-watchers.

29

The barred owl is widespread in North America, occurring in a wide range of wooded habitats, including swamp forests. This owl has caught a frog in a bed of water hyacinths growing in a woodland pool.

Ural Owl

Measuring 60 centimetres (24 inches) in length, the Ural owl *(Strix uralensis)* is only marginally smaller than the great grey owl, which it superficially resembles. It lacks the concentric rings which mark the latter's facial disc, and in many ways resembles an outsized tawny owl. The main range of the Ural owl is from northern Europe eastward into Siberia, but it does occur in isolated populations in the mountains of south-central Europe. Like its larger relative, it too feeds mainly on small mammals and will also attack intruders near its nest, usually deliberately aiming its blows at the face and eyes.

Barred Owl

The barred owl *(Strix varia)* is widespread and comparatively common in North America, occurring across most of the eastern half of the continent from Florida northward to southern Canada; it is also spreading westward in the north of its range, and already occurs in Washington State. It is a medium-sized owl, 50 centimetres (20 inches) or so in length, with attractively marked brown plumage and, as its name denotes, extensive barring.

Barred owls are woodland birds that prefer mixed or coniferous forests. In much of their range they are almost exclusively nocturnal and only seen during the daytime when disturbed. Visitors to reserves in southern Florida often encounter them during the day, however, for the owls seemingly have acquired that most striking character of this state's birdlife: tameness.

The Ural owl is one of Europe's most magnificent species. Although superficially similar to the great grey owl, it lacks the dark concentric rings seen on that species' facial disc.

Spotted Owl

Amongst conservationist and logging circles, the spotted owl *(Strix occidentalis)* is a byword for controversy. It has come to symbolise the fight against clear-cut commercial logging of old-growth forests in America's Pacific north-west, a habitat upon which this species is entirely dependent. Spotted owls are now very rare and entirely protected by law. The greatest damage to the species may, however, already have been done since so much forest has all but disappeared. Spotted owls seem reluctant to venture across unsuitable habitats, so populations isolated in pockets of remaining forest seem destined to lose contact with others of the same species from elsewhere within their range.

Spotted owls are superficially similar to the more widespread and common barred owl. As one might expect, however, the main distinction lies in its plumage, which displays pale spots rather than dark bars.

Long-eared Owl

The long-eared owl *(Asio otus)* is extremely widespread in the northern hemisphere, occurring across Europe, Asia, and much of North America. The owl's most prominent features are its long 'ear' tufts, which are raised or lowered according to the bird's mood. Although they may resemble true ears, the tufts are in fact extended feathers and have no role to play in hearing.

Long-eared owls are strictly nocturnal, feeding mainly on small mammals during the breeding season; in the winter they will occasionally take birds such as thrushes. The nest usually belonged to a crow, abandoned in dense conifer woodland. In the winter long-eared owls usually disperse and move southward; they will sometimes roost communally in certain areas.

Best known for the controversy it arouses in conservation circles, the spotted owl is North America's most endangered owl. It lives exclusively in old-growth forests in the Pacific north-west, a habitat which has suffered tremendously from clear-cutting.

Long-eared owls are so-called because of the long feather tufts on the head. These have no function in hearing, however; the true ears are concealed by feathers at the edge of the owl's facial disc.

Saw-whet Owl

Named thus because its call is supposed to resemble the sound of a saw being sharpened, the saw-whet owl *(Aegolius acadicus)* is widespread in North America. It is a compact and rather rounded owl, only 20 centimetres (8 inches) or so in length. The plumage is reddish brown and the eyes are yellow and staring. When found in the winter months, saw-whet owls are often confiding and approachable; when nesting, they are considerably more secretive and wary.

Boobook Owl

Named for its double-note call, the boobook owl *(Ninox novaeseelandiae)* is widespread in Australia and New Zealand. Although primarily a woodland species, it is found increasingly in mature gardens and sometimes in towns and cities. The owl is rather slender, an appearance often accentuated by its upright posture when perched on a fence post or gate. The plumage is dark brown with darker streaking on the paler underparts. Boobook owls are nocturnal; they feed mainly on insects, but occasionally enjoy a lizard or small mammal.

Short-eared Owl

Because of its partly diurnal habits and preference for open country, the short-eared owl *(Asio flammeus)* is one of the most commonly seen species. It hunts by quartering up and down over grassy areas in search of small mammals such as voles and mice; small birds will also be taken if the opportunity arises.

Short-eared owls are one of the few larger birds to benefit from conifer plantations in their early stages. These provide both feeding and nesting habitat, since this species invariably nests on the ground.

Hawk Owl

The hawk owl *(Surnia ulula)* is one of the least typical of all the owls. In many ways it bears more than a passing resemblance to the bird of prey for which it is named, due in part to its elongated shape, particularly its tail. It is also essentially diurnal in habits, and perches on prominent look-out posts, continually scanning the terrain for prey.

Hawk owls are northern birds associated during the breeding season with the boreal forests of North America, northern Europe, and Asia. Their precise distribution from year to year is rather unpredictable and influenced strongly by the abundance or absence of voles and the other small mammals that comprise its diet. During the winter months hawk owls disperse and generally move southward in search of winter feeding.

More like a diurnal raptor than an owl, the northern hawk owl feeds mainly by day. It uses look-out perches to watch for likely prey animals that include birds and small mammals.

SILENT HUNTERS

While eagles, hawks, falcons, and other birds of prey have become the dominant diurnal predators, owls have a near monopoly on this feeding strategy after dark. The twilight hours of dawn and dusk are their domain, as well as the dead of night, when no other avian predators can function. Excellent senses of sight and hearing are essential prerequisites for this lifestyle. The hunting strategy of owls also differs from most birds of prey in another fundamental way. Diurnal raptors often use speed or surprise to get close enough to their quarry for the kill. Owls, on the other hand, rely on silent flight to come upon their prey by stealth: they are the silent hunters of the night.

Wings and Feathers

Most people who have examined a road-casualty owl are amazed by how much of the apparent body size is comprised of feathering and how little the bird itself weighs. Couple this with the usually broad and expansive wings, and it is not surprising that owls are capable of buoyant and leisurely flight. This in itself is enough to reduce the sound of flapping wings, but owls have an additional feature that creates almost silent flight, namely feather design to muffle wind flow.

When held up to the light the flight feathers of most birds show a clean edge. Those of owls, however, are rather different. The leading edge of these feathers, together with the outer third or so of the trailing edge, are armed with a bristly fringe which has the effect of silencing any rush of air. Additionally, the upper surface of the outer flight feathers has a rather downy texture which also serves to muffle the sound.

The silent flight of owls serves two main purposes, both of which relate to their hunting lifestyle. Firstly, it enables them to take by surprise prey such as small mammals which have an acute sense of hearing. Secondly, by reducing any background noise it assists the owls' own sense of hearing, a vital component of any species' hunting ability.

An owl's eyes are protected by a nictitating membrane which can be closed at will. The motion of the membrane also serves to remove dust and debris caught on the surface of the eye.

Small mammals form a major part of the diet of the saw-whet owl. The prey is usually carried to a convenient perch where it is swallowed whole. The ground beneath a regularly used perch may be whitewashed with droppings.

Silent flight helps owls—for instance, this long-eared owl—in two ways. First it allows them to approach their prey without detection, and also it cuts down background noise, allowing them to hear sounds from their quarry without interference.

Silently dropping like a stone from its lookout perch, this spotted owl will catch an unsuspecting mouse on the forest floor in the next instant. The sharp talons will probably kill the mouse with a single blow.

Owls have flight feathers modified for silent flight. The leading edges, as well as the outer margin of the trailing edges, have projections that help muffle sound.

Meticulous preening keeps the flight feathers of this saw-whet owl in perfect order. Its flight is relatively silent due to an adaptation in the structure of the feathers themselves.

Following page: Dawn and dusk are when the little owl is most active. It is at these times of day that the birds are most vocal and when their weird, catlike calls can be heard.

Vision

Look into the face of any owl and you will be left in little doubt that vision is important to these birds. Huge staring eyes will fix their gaze upon you, giving the bird an air of benign wisdom or malevolent hatred, depending on the owl's mood. The eyesight of owls is legendary, particularly their ability to see in near darkness. Recent studies have shown, however, that their vision is not quite as acute as was once supposed. It would appear, in fact, that the combination of an owl's vision and hearing work in harmony.

An owl's eyes are, in effect, fixed in their sockets. They face forward and provide a wide angle of vision, the overlapping field of view providing binocular, stereoscopic vision. Having eyes fixed in their sockets could prove a disadvantage when it comes to scanning the surroundings. To compensate for this, owls have evolved incredibly flexible necks that enable the birds to rotate their heads 360 degrees, or even turn them upside down.

The eyes are also adapted for seeing at low light intensities, with large pupils and a retina (the layer of light-receptive cells at the back of the lens) endowed with a greater proportion of cells than diurnal birds. These extremely sensitive cells, called rods, enable the owl to see only in monochrome. Although owls' eyes are undoubtedly more acute at low light levels than our own, it is probably only by a factor of three or four times that they differ.

Hearing

Many owls, such as the long-eared owl or great horned owl, have what appear to be conspicuous ear tufts on their heads. Despite their appearance, however, these have nothing whatsoever to do with hearing. The ears instead are concealed by feathering at the margins of the facial disc. The openings of the ears are very large and they are also placed asymmetrically—one higher than the other when the owl's face is viewed head on. This heightens the bird's ability to pinpoint a sound source, both in terms of direction and of distance.

An owl's staring eyes are its most striking feature. They are surrounded by a facial disc, the outer borders of which cover the openings of the ears.

Owls are able to alter their shape markedly by stretching or contracting their bodies and flattening or fluffing up their feathers. This short-eared owl looks surprisingly elongated, after having been agitated for some reason.

Beak and Talons

All owls have relatively long legs and large feet which are equipped with fearsome talons. It is these that enable the bird to capture the prey; the grip and the piercing bite of the talons are often enough to deliver a fatal blow along with the first strike. Under normal circumstances three toes are carried facing forward with one facing backward, and this is sufficient for perching. At times, however, the outer toe can be reversed and this greatly enhances the prey-capturing capability of the feet.

Like diurnal birds of prey, all owls have a long, hook-tipped beak. This is sometimes used to kill prey held in the talons, but is more often used to carry prey in flight or to tear portions off larger quarry prior to swallowing or feeding to young. Much of the beak is concealed by feathering and therefore can appear quite small. When opened wide for swallowing, however, a huge gape is revealed, more than enough for most owl species to swallow a small mammal whole.

A barred owl alights on its quarry in the grass. The owl lands talons-first, by which the bird delivers the fatal blow to the victim.

The base of an owl's bill is cloaked in feathering. Only when the bird opens its mouth wide to swallow prey is the true extent of its gape revealed.

Owls possess four toes on their feet. Under normal circumstances three usually point forward and one points to the rear. When perching, however, one of the forward-facing toes can be reversed to provide better stability.

A ghostly shape swoops silently through the rafters of an old farm building. This barn owl has taken up residence here and may even breed in years to come.

Small prey items are usually swallowed whole by owls. With larger quarry, however, the feet and talons grip the victim, which is then torn and dismembered by the sharp bill.

A great grey owl in flight is an impressive sight as it skims low over the ground in a wintery landscape. When snow blankets the land, feeding may become extremely difficult for these large birds.

A tawny owl carries a young rabbit back to its nest in a hole in a tree. Here it will be dismembered and fed to the owl's ravenous offspring.

Diet and Feeding

Many owl species, even surprisingly large-sized ones, feed almost exclusively on small mammals, and this is clearly the feeding strategy that suits the group as a whole. There are, however, a number of notable exceptions. Many of the smaller owls, especially those from warmer climates, specialise in catching insects while, at the other extreme, eagle owls have been known to tackle prey the size of a small deer.

Perhaps the most unusual diet is found in the fishing owls and fish owls which, as their names relate, capture fish.

Among the diurnal birds of prey some species, notably vultures, have specialised in feeding on carrion. There are no owls that have adopted this way of life. Most owls feed almost exclusively on the prey to which they are best adapted and show little variation in their feeding preferences. However, species which have a particularly wide global distribution are sometimes more adaptable. The short-eared owl, for example, is a specialist in small-mammal feeding within much of its range in the northern hemisphere, but on the Galápagos Islands in the Pacific Ocean, this diet is not a viable option. Instead, island owls feed almost exclusively on storm petrels as they come and go from their breeding colonies.

Owls hunt in two primary ways. Species such as barn owls and short-eared owls often quarter areas of grass with slow, buoyant flight, looking and listening for the movements of voles and mice below. Others, such as the forest-dwelling species, prefer to perch motionless on a lookout branch, watching and listening for the tell-tale signs of prey below.

Larger species of owls often swallow their prey whole or divide it into more-or-less intact portions. The food is eaten, but the bones and often the fur or feathers of the victims are indigestible. From time to time owls regurgitate pellets containing said matter, and this frequent function is often performed at a regular site. Pellets can, therefore, be collected and a good assessment of the owl's diet can be made. In order to examine a pellet yourself, soak it for a short while in water before teasing it apart.

The diet of many owls is not confined simply to small mammals and birds; many species are opportunistic feeders. This screech owl has just caught a frog.

NESTING AND REARING YOUNG

For owls, as with other birds, the period during which nesting and rearing young occurs is the most important part of the annual cycle. It is the time during which genes are passed on to the next generation, and considerable effort is expended by the parents in this respect. In the case of most owl species, especially those found in temperate or sub-Arctic regions, breeding occurs during the spring. However, all the upbringing of their young, and the period immediately following their fledging, is invariably timed to coincide with the maximum abundance of prey animals.

Monogamy

As a general rule owls are monogamous, that is to say pairs are comprised of one male and one female, neither one of which has any involvement with other nesting birds. This is in contrast to some species of

passerine birds where a single male may mate with more than one female, and take partial responsibility for the upbringing of several broods. The reverse case—wherein one female mates with several males—is less commonly observed among birds. With some owl species the pair bonds last only for the duration of the breeding season, especially if the species involved is dispersive or migratory.

Unlike its parents this snowy owl chick does not have white plumage. Instead, it is covered with greyish down which affords it a degree of camouflage against the tundra when its parents are absent from the nest.

Lemmings form an important part of the diet of young snowy owls. In years when lemming numbers are poor, few, if any, of the chicks are likely to survive.

Owls will often use any available lookout perch to scan for potential prey. This snowy owl is using a low-growing conifer on the fringes of the Arctic tundra.

Having just captured a small mammal, this burrowing owl is shrouding its victim with its wings in a display known as 'mantling'. Many other owl species show this particular behaviour.

They vigourously defend the nest and a well-defined, surrounding feeding territory against members of the same species and other birds that might conceivably compete for the same resources. If the owls are dispersive, this territoriality lasts only for the duration of the breeding season. Year-round residents such as tawny owls and eagle owls will defend their territories throughout the year, their efforts extending to offspring of the previous year once they are more than a few months past fledging. Attacks on intruders are invariably uninhibited and vicious if the intruder stands its ground. Smaller owl species—potential competitors for food and nesting sites—are also attacked, and tawny owls, for example, will readily kill long-eared owls in their territory; this effectively results in the fact that two species do not overlap in terms of their precise distributions.

In others, particularly sedentary species such as the little owl, pairs may remain together throughout the year. Tawny owl pairs are similarly faithful to one another, their bonds remaining for life.

Territoriality

Owls are territorial, a fact that is particularly evident during the breeding season.

Diurnal species of owls will sometimes advertise their territories in a visual manner. Thus short-eared owls perform buoyant-flight and wing-clapping displays to announce their presence to other birds, both potential mates and intruders. Nocturnal species of owls invariably use sound as a means of advertisement. The calls of

This burrowing owl spreads its wings to increase its size and thus makes itself seem more threatening. This owl's alarm call sounds rather like a rattlesnake, a creature which itself can pose a threat to the owls when nesting.

Despite its comparatively small size, this burrowing owl is showing threatening behaviour toward an intruder. Most owls are fearless when it comes to defending their nests from attack.

sedentary species often involve duets between established pairs, rather than individual birds.

Nest Sites

In the strict sense of the word, owls do not construct nests in the same way as songbirds do. Instead they are opportunistic nesters, using ready-made sites or taking over the abandoned nests of other birds.

Owl species that breed in open terrain are often ground nesters. The snowy owl, which favours the Arctic tundra, will use a hollow in the ground which the female may attempt to scrape out and line with plant material. Short-eared owls often nest in or beside tussocks of grass; similar sites are sometimes chosen on rare occasions by long-eared owls and tawny owls, both usually tree-nesting species.

Holes in trees are another preferred site for a wide variety of owls, and a few species, notably the barn owl, have adopted the man-made equivalent of these sites—namely, holes in barns and other outbuildings. The abandoned nests of crows and birds of prey are also favoured by many owl species, with sometimes little or no attempt to embellish the previous owner's construction. Lastly, natural rock crevices or ledges are used by a few species, including that most impressive of owls, the eagle owl.

Eggs and Nestlings

Owls lay between one and thirteen eggs, depending on the species and also on the particular season; for most, however, three or four is the more common number. The eggs are rounded and white; there is little need for cryptic markings given the concealed nature of most nest sites, and the vigour with which they are defended.

Incubation of the eggs usually begins when the first one is laid, and lasts, in most species, for around thirty days. Because eggs are laid over a period of several days, the hatching is also staggered. This means that there is always a gradation in the size of the chicks in the nest, the larger and more active individuals invariably getting more food from the parents than their smaller, weaker siblings. As a result, it is

Following page: With feathers ruffled and wings spread, these young great horned owls put on an impressive threat display toward intruders. If the intrusion were to continue the parents would soon come to their rescue.

From the security of its nest in a hole in a tree, this saw-whet owl stares back confidently at intruders. Very few creatures can threaten a nest in such an in-vulnerable site.

The hollow trunk of an oak tree provides an ideal nest site for these tawny owl chicks. Before too long they will leave the nest and be cared for and fed by the adults in the surrounding woodland.

The staring eyes and gaping hooked bill of this short-eared owl are enough to intimidate most creatures that would threaten its nest.

The marsh owl is the African equivalent of the short-eared owl of Eurasia and North America. As its name relates, it favours extensive marshes and swamps and occurs mainly south of the Sahara.

Apparently posing for the camera, these two burrowing owl chicks stand outside their nest burrow catching the evening sun. Such behaviour is not uncommon in this species.

This spotted eagle owl is returning to its nest in a hollow tree, carrying a large snake. Reptiles form an important part of the diet of many owl species, especially those from the tropics.

In their first few days of life owlets are almost completely helpless. The eyes of these hatchlings have barely opened, and were it not for their secure nest site and the attentions of their parents, they would be vulnerable to attack.

Essentially a ground-nesting species, the short-eared owl is often called upon to aggressively defend its young against attack from terrestrial predators. In this respect its sharp talons serve it well.

Four chicks in a great grey owl nest is a good number for this species. Unless food is particularly plentiful, one or more of them will not reach the fledging stage, as the larger chicks monopolise the feeding attentions of the adults.

Saw-whet owl youngsters are almost comical to look at, as their heads seem disproportionately large for their bodies. Their cuddly appearance, however, belies their ability to inflict painful wounds on any creature that threatens them.

Great grey owls are renowned for the ferocious vigour with which they defend their nests and young. Humans who stray too near a nest site are unhesitatingly attacked with the full force of the owl's talons.

One of a pair of screech owl youngsters calls for the attention of its parents. It seems images like this are made for comical captions!

rare for all the chicks that hatch from a clutch to survive, except of course when food is plentiful. In most seasons the youngest chicks starve, or are sometimes even killed by their brothers or sisters. This seemingly brutal approach to the rearing of young has in fact positive survival advantages for the family as a whole: it ensures that, whatever the food availability, some offspring will always survive and produce further offspring. If all the young were fed equally there would be a chance that all might starve in years of poor food supply.

Defending the Nest

However callous the parent owls' approach to feeding their offspring may appear, they cannot be criticised for their courage in defending the nest. Many of the medium-sized and large species will unhesitatingly attack even a human that strays too close, often directing blows with the feet and talons at the intruder's face and eyes. There are well-documented cases of people losing an eye due to tawny owl attacks, and the ferocity of a great grey owl at its nest is nearly legendary.

Whatever the weather, nests are guarded and chicks incubate. This great horned owl is panting in an attempt to cool off on a sunny day.

This row of screech owl chicks presents an endearing sight. It may take two weeks or more before they are fully independent, during which time they are fed and guarded by the parents.

Hunting is a skill that improves with experience. This juvenile great grey owl has just made an undignified crash-landing, missing the small mammal it intended to catch.

This great horned owl has nested in an abandoned crow's nest. This species is less retiring than most other owls, its confidence heightened by its large size and ability to defend itself.

The great horned owl is the most wide-ranging species in the Americas and also the least habitat specific. This one is occupying a nest in a huge cactus in the deserts of Arizona.

OWLS TODAY

As a group, owls have representatives in almost all parts of the world where potential prey animals are found, offering tempting prospects for keen bird-watchers everywhere. Their often nocturnal habits can make them difficult to observe, but for many people this only serves as a challenge, the pleasure heightened all the more for the degree of difficulty in locating and seeing them.

For some, the prospect of finding a nocturnal bird that hides itself during the hours of daylight may seem daunting. However, there are often clues that can assist the observer, and knowing the habits and habitat requirements of the species in question can greatly improve the chances of success. The first part of this chapter deals with some of the most important bird-watching regions around the world, subdivided into habitats or regions where appropriate.

North America

The tundra and boreal forests harbour some of North America's most spectacular species. On the open tundra the huge snowy owl is the dominant avian predator, feeding mainly on lemmings; visit Nome or Barrow in Alaska for the best chances of seeing birds during the summer months. At lower latitudes boreal forests predominate and this is home to the hawk owl. Its habit of perching high on a lookout tree make it comparatively easy to locate, although its numbers and distribution vary from year to year; best chances of observation are in central Alaska. Also at home in

Seemingly oblivious to the sharp spines that armour this cactus, the tiny elf owl perches for a while during its nighttime foray. This species, from the deserts of the southern United States and Central America, is entirely nocturnal.

this habitat is the great grey owl, North America's largest owl. Despite its size it can be difficult to find; watch along forest rides at dawn and dusk.

Throughout North America's temperate forests a variety of owl species can be found. The largest of these is the great horned owl, best known for its calls. Smaller and more

The extraordinary facial appearance of the spectacled owl gives the species its name. A secretive tropical bird from Central and South America, it is heard more often than it is seen.

A pair of spotted owls rest in a forest of old-growth trees in America's Pacific north-west. With the species becoming ever rarer, this is an increasingly unusual sight.

A migratory summer visitor to the region, the flammulated owl is found in the south-eastern portion of the United States. It favours ponderosa pine woodlands, where its hooting call gives away its presence.

secretive is the long-eared owl, which is often easier to find in winter when they may roost communally, and the ground beneath their tree roost becomes white-washed with droppings and littered with pellets. Saw-whet owls and screech owls also favour this habitat.

Grassland and open country is the pre-ferred habitat of the short-eared owl, a species which often hunts during daylight hours. Scanning across open habitats with binoculars can be productive; the observer should pay particular attention to fence posts, upon which the owls frequently perch. Barn owls also favour this habitat, common only in the western half of the United States; they are largely nocturnal in their habits.

Florida offers excellent opportunities for observing two owl species in particular. Burrowing owls sometimes nest right beside roads, using burrows in excavated soil. They also occupy rabbit burrows on golf courses; the owls of Marathon Key golf course, for

In winter, food shortages may force Tengmalm's (boreal) owls to extend their range southward. Hunger may also force them to feed openly during daylight hours at this time of year.

Tengmalm's owls find feeding difficult when the winter snows arrive. If the weather is particularly severe, they may be forced to fly south to milder regions.

example, are well known. Barred owls are also much easier to see in this state than elsewhere in the United States, and the Audubon Society's Corkscrew Swamp Sanctuary is particularly good for such observing. The diminutive elf owl is a specialty of saguaro cactus deserts in southern Arizona, New Mexico, and Texas.

Almost all the owls of northern latitudes in North America move southward for winter to avoid the worst temperatures and in order to find food, the precise winter location depending on these factors. Many of the boreal owls make it as far south as the northern United States. Snowy owls, for example, regularly turn up on the eastern seaboard coastal marshes as far south as Cape Cod, Massachusetts.

Central and South America

Although there are plenty of owl species that occur in tropical forests, the chances of actually seeing any are rather remote. Visitors to one of the forest reserves in Costa Rica or the Llanos region of Venezuela, for instance, might be lucky enough to glimpse—or more likely simply hear—a crested owl or a spectacled owl; the calls of the former are gruff and froglike while those of the latter are deep, a sort of thumping boom.

Visitors to the Galápagos Islands in the Pacific Ocean will probably not have the opportunity to see a short-eared owl, given the species' widespread global distribution. Here, however, the owls are incredibly tame and often sit around on rocks in broad daylight.

Following page: During the winter months short-eared owls move southward from their breeding range. They may concentrate in areas where prey animals such as mice and voles are particularly numerous.

Europe

Like North America, Europe's grasslands are home to both short-eared owls and barn owls. The latter are scarce but widespread, while the former breed in northern regions and migrate south in winter.

Europe's most common woodland owl is the tawny owl. Although nocturnal and comparatively shy, it is extremely vocal at dusk and can often be located by tracing the source of its loud hoots. During the daytime listen for woodland songbirds mobbing roosting owls.

Like North America, the more northern latitudes have a fair number of boreal nesting species. Finland has perhaps the greatest diversity, with hawk owls, great grey owls, Ural owls, and Tengmalm's owls. Beyond the tree line the tundra is the domain of the snowy owl, whose range has extended as far southward as the Shetland Isles off the coast of Scotland.

Olive groves around the Mediterranean are the home of the little owl, which is often seen during the day. Its range, extending northward in Europe as far as southern Britain, also plays host to the delightful Scops owl, whose sonar-blip call is a most familiar sound.

Africa

Game drives in many of the East African game parks can sometimes provide opportunities to observe species such as the pearl-spotted owlet and Verreaux's eagle owl at their daytime roosts. The latter use regular sites in acacia trees, and these are sometimes well known to local guides. The owlets are very vocal at night and sometimes can be heard calling near wooded campsites.

Asia

Observing owls in Asia is more of a challenge than in most other parts of the world. Spotted owlets are sometimes found roosting during the day in areas of open country or farmland; the wetland reserve of Bharatpur in India, for example, is fine for observing this species. Collared Scops owls are found in similar habitats, as are mottled wood owls.

Australia and New Zealand

Australia has an excellent network of national parks and reserves, many of which have park rangers who can assist with requests for information. Without too much difficulty, visitors to the eastern half of the continent, particularly east of the Great Dividing Range, should be able to see or hear powerful owls, barking owls, and the ubiquitous boobook owl. The easiest owl to observe in New Zealand is the unappealingly named morepork, named for its unusual call; it is related to the Australian boobook owl.

A Eurasian pygmy owl rests on a conifer branch in central Europe. This species is active during the day and feeds mainly on birds. Although comparatively small it is fearless when defending its nest and young.

A marsh owl flies low over a marsh in search of prey such as amphibians and small mammals. Unlike most owls, this species will often be seen feeding during daylight hours.

Fortunate visitors to South and East Africa may see a Verreaux's eagle owl while on safari. This one is roosting in the shade of an acacia tree, a site which it regularly uses.

Despite its small size this Austral pygmy owl from southern Chile is a fearless predator of small birds. It feeds during daylight and is comparatively easy to observe.

To see a Verreaux's eagle owl in broad daylight is not a particularly unusual sight. This one was photographed in the Kruger National Park in South Africa.

Known in Europe and Asia as Tengmalm's owl, and in North America as the boreal owl, this species breeds at high latitudes. Abandoned woodpecker holes are often favoured nesting sites.

These spotted eagle owls from Africa are resting in the shade of a bush during the heat of the day. Not until dusk, when it is markedly cooler, will the owls emerge to hunt.

Threats Facing Owls Today

Owls, like many groups of birds around the world today, face a number of threats and new challenges to their survival. While deliberate persecution does not present the same dangers that it once did, habitat loss or degradation undoubtedly poses the most serious threat. Despite this, however, comparatively few species of owls (with the exception of the spotted owl, noted earlier) are in grave danger, and there are plenty of places around the world where they can be observed.

Countless generations of people have revered and appreciated owls for their beauty and elegance, as well as for their perceived wisdom and intelligence. Let us hope that we will also show some enlightened behaviour when it comes to preserving the habitats necessary for owls and other wildlife to survive. By accomplishing this, future generations too can be thrilled by the glare of an owl's great, staring eyes, or be awestruck by the sight of this remarkable bird flying silently through the night.

This long-eared owl has chosen an abandoned crow's nest in which to lay its eggs and rear its young. Long-eared owls are strictly nocturnal and remain in deep cover during the daytime.

Standing more than 60 centimetres (2 feet) tall, the eagle owl is a magnificent sight. The ear tufts on its head are not used in hearing, however; its true ears lie at the margins of the facial disc.

INDEX

Page numbers in **bold-face** type indicate photo captions.